·THE·
EAT YOUR OWN PET
·COOKBOOK·

Russell Jones

GRUB STREET LONDON

. . . .

The author lives in East London where
he shares a flat with ⚡1 cat,
⚡2 budgies and 1 very large dog who
bites him regularly

Dedicated to Debbie and Hannah

With thanks to John the Spiv and Karen

•

Published in Great Britain in 1988 by
Grub Street, Golden House
28–31 Great Pulteney Street
London W1R 3DD

Copyright © Grub Street
Copyright Text and illustrations © Russell Jones

Jones, Russell
The eat your own pet cookbook
I. Title
828: 91409
ISBN 0–948817–23–2

Typeset by Chapterhouse, Formby, England
Printed in Great Britain by Maclehose and Partners

CONTENTS

INTRODUCTION

Welcome to the wonderful world of domestic pet eating! Over the years this twilit corner of rich culinary delights has been sadly neglected. The reasons for this are diverse. Attachment to say, the family cat, or consideration for a small child struggling with tiny hands to keep it's squealing Christmas present out of the roasting pan, or just a plain old fashioned reluctance to branch out into the untried and exotic — all these have prevented many people from joining the munching ranks of pet lovers.

As a committed indulger of many years standing, I've wined and

dined on everything from the humble Rat in a Basket (page 18) to the complex 101 Dalmations with 76 Trombones Pomme Flambé (page 41) and can think of no finer sight than a huge steaming hound carcass lying defeated but still proud on a bed of wild rice. I'm sure you'll agree. If so, the time has come for me to give you the benefit of my knowledge and experience.

Within these pages you'll find everything you need to know. Not only mouth-watering recipes but a wealth of priceless information, such as how to choose your pet wisely, special equipment you may need, and a few tried and tested methods of squaring the sudden disappearance of the family pet with the kids. There are even handy hints on putting them to sleep in a painless and tasteful way, along with many tips and pointers towards happy, wholesome family munching.

So! Cast away your irrational devotion to domestic fur and feather with one hand and pick up this book with the other! Gather up your utensils and step with me into the heady world of pet cuisine. Read on and remember when next time your cat-flap opens and that familiar furry head peers into your kitchen, don't think cat — think calories!

Bon Appetit

Russell Jones

WET NOSE

TIMID.
DISPOSITION

APPEALING NATURE

CUDDLY DEMEANOUR

CUTE
LOOKS

GOOD
CHOPPERS

BRIGHT
EYES

BUSHY
TAIL

SPOTTING A SQUARE MEAL

That the raw ingredients in pet cuisine are of the highest importance cannot be stressed too strongly, so always opt for the pet that's been well cared for, even pampered. As a general rule the cute, cuddlesome little Yorkshire Terrier in the tartan overcoat and silk bow will make a far better dish than the aloof, skulking mongrel from a deprived background.

Look for these reassuring signs. Bright eyes, bushy tail, good choppers, timid disposition, cuddly demeanour, cute looks, wet nose, and appealing nature.

Seek out that unmistakable 'I'm man's best friend look', written all over a face, and you won't go far wrong.

SOME SPECIAL EQUIPMENT

❶ CAT-FLAP GUILLOTINE

❷ PEA GREEN RELIANT THREE-WHEELER

❸ CANARY'S DOME OF DOOM

1. Place accoustically opaque dome over cage, ignoring all protests from the occupant. Bolt fast (fig 2).
2. Load revolvers and fire.
3. Remove Dome of Doom.

(Note: In the unlikely event of the occupant surviving, reload and repeat process.)

❹ 17 FT. STEAMBOAT

Especially suitable for 101 Dalmations recipe (see page 41)

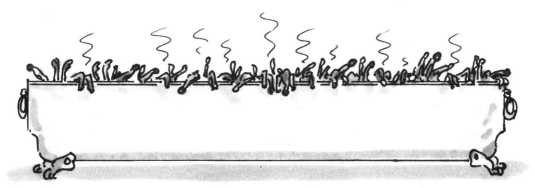

FIVE GOOD REASONS FOR DOING ' EM IN

I present here five classic and persuasive reasons for overcoming any irrational attachment some of you may have to the household pet, in the hope that even the more sensitive amongst you may be encouraged to despatch them into a state of 'premature, permanent hibernation'.

1. The horror of discovering half way through the 1812 Overture that the cat has pooed in your headphones.

YOU 'ORRIBLE, HYPOCRITICAL FOUR EYED, BALD HEADED TOSSPOT!!

2. The blistering embarrassment you feel as the parrot decides to vent its spleen on an honoured guest.

3. The nights of misery when the hamster decides to work out on the wheel.

4. The heart stopping shock as your daughter's pony unloads a rosegrower's dream into the back of your '58 convertible.

5. The numbing pain as that psychopathic pile of feathers known as your budgie pecks playfully at your finger.

PUTTING YOUR PET TO SLEEP

Despatching fur or feather to that "Great Menagerie in the Sky" need not be the messy unpleasant business it once was.

Indeed, it can be fun for all the family as the illustration depicting the decline and fall of a sleeping Tom, clearly shows.

Step 1. Make sure the mogg is soundly asleep. Nose twitching is a good indicator of this condition.

Step 2. Smite the gong a hefty blow.

Step 3. Stand well back and the beast will rise gracefully into the air. Heights of four or even five metres are not uncommon.

Step 4. On returning to ground level, heart failure should be complete. The Tom, having been removed swiftly and painlessly to the 'other side', is now ready for preparation.

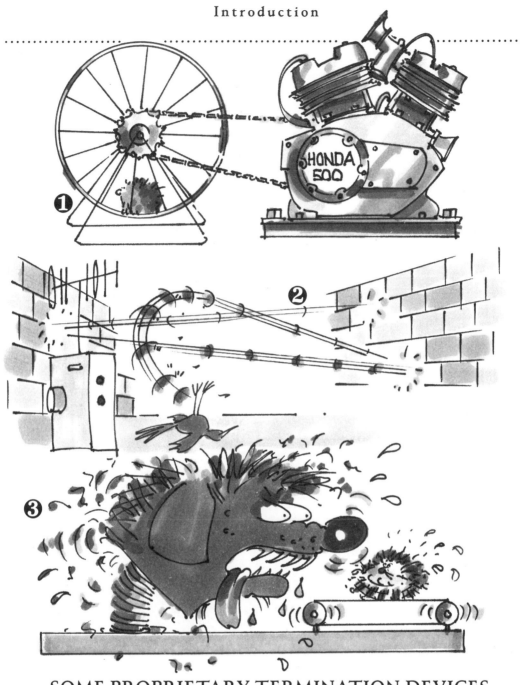

SOME PROPRIETARY TERMINATION DEVICES

Should you still wish to distance yourself from what you may wrongly consider an unpleasant task, there are several patented machines on the market, three of which are shown above.

1. The ever popular Hamster's Wheel of Misfortune.

2. The North by South-west Infrared Homing Pigeon Direction Scrambler.
3. The Acme Industries Small Rodent Exhauster.

Other methods especially suitable for the larger animal can be found throughout this book or a full list can be had by writing directly to *Fur 'n' Feather Quarterly.*

SOUPS AND

We begin our journey into pet cuisine with that classic starter, Turine of Tortoise in it's Shell. Detailed below is a handy if somewhat cruel method of despatching the animal into the world beyond, commonly known as '**The Run with a Walkman Method**'.

... ANY WUN OOOH 'AD AN 'ART ...

You'll require a Sony Walkman and a Very Best of Cilla tape. Place the headphones on shell, turn the volume to full and stand clear.

SONY

The animal in its frantic but futile efforts to escape the offending sounds will reach speeds to which tortoise are unaccustomed.

... WOULD LOOKER MEEEE...

The result of which will be total, irreversible exhaustion.

.. AN' KNOW THA' RI LUV YER.

WARNING: WHEN USING THIS METHOD WE STRONGLY RECOMMEND THE USE OF GOOD QUALITY EAR DEFENDERS OR THE PROCESS COULD BACK-FIRE ON YOU!

STARTERS

TURINE OF TORTOISE IN IT'S SHELL

INGREDIENTS

To serve 4 adults

1 4lb (2kg) Tortoise

1 large turnip

½ gallon (2 litres) of tortoise stock

handful of parsley

handful of chilli

METHOD

Slowly boil tortoise in stock together with turnip, half the parsley and half the chilli. When cooked toss in all the remaining ingredients and serve in it's shell. Decorate with the headphones.

HANDY HINT: As tortoise can be very tough and leathery we recommend 1 day's cooking for each year of age. As some can live to be 30 or 40, this is not an ideal dish for a quick mid-morning snack. Nor is it, even if the cooking times are strictly adhered to, a dish for wearers of false teeth.

We move on to another majestic dish, Goldfish Gumbo and below an equally legendary method of getting them out of the bowl, into the pan.

Goldfish are timid creatures and will often respond favourably to threats of intimidation. the technique shown here owes much to the North Atlantic U-Boat war of the 1940's and to its principal weapon, the depth charge.

No mess, no fuss and based entirely on deceit and fabrication, this method can be lots of fun for all the family.

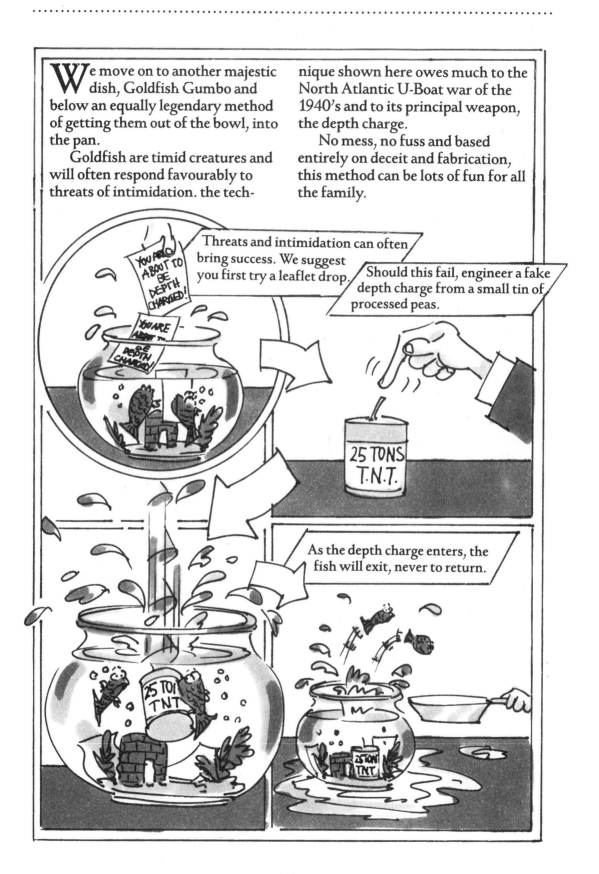

GOLDFISH GUMBO OR "BELLY-UP BISQUE"

HOW MANY OF us have wandered back from the fairground having spent the equivalent of the gross national product trying to win a prize by shooting a moving line of little tin ducks with an air gun, the barrel of which has more bends in it then a country road. All of us I suspect — and what do we have to show for it? Empty pockets and a tiny polythene bag containing a couple of startled-looking goldfish. Don't despair! Reach for a saucepan, and console yourself that you're about to eat the world's most expensive soup.

INGREDIENTS

To serve 3 hungry children

2 goldfish	1 leek
1 large onion	2 carrots
	salt and pepper, to taste

METHOD

Prepare fish and together with finely chopped vegetables place into 1 pint of boiling, salted water. Simmer for 25 minutes. Serve in a glass bowl for authenticity, making sure the fish are belly-up. If eating outdoors, cool and serve individual portions in small polythene bags.

KITTEN CRUNCH

KITTEN CRUNCH IS a crisp creation that characterises the craft of the crack, creative cook. More crunchy than crusty bread, more crumbly than crackers it's a crazy concoction when criss-crossed with cress, crimped and crammed on a crumpet.

INGREDIENTS

To serve 1

1 kitten	4 crumpets
2 lb (1 kg) potatoes	2 oz (50g) dripping
handful of cress	2 lemons

METHOD

Draw and truss kitten, spread with dripping and place in oven at 325°F (160°C), Gas Mark 3. Boil potatoes and place around kitten in roasting pan and cook for three hours. When all is crisp and even, remove and garnish with cherries, squirt with lemon juice and serve with cress and a crumpet.

RAT IN A BASKET

THIS RECIPE WAS the original "Ploughman's Lunch" and was supplied by the more thoughtful landowner for his workers, toiling in the fields many years ago. So generous were some amongst the landed gentry, they charged the peasant only half price for the food at Christmas.

Cheap and cheerful, this recipe is ideal as a packed lunch and should be enjoyed with a glass of beer and a good yarn.

INGREDIENTS

To serve 1

1 or 2 medium size pet rats	1 bottle cooking oil
2 lb (1kg) potatoes	salt and pepper, to taste
1 lb (500g) breadcrumbs	

METHOD

Prepare and dress rats and coat with oil and breadcrumbs. Peel and chip potatoes, place with rats in a chip pan and deep fry until crisp. Remove and arrange in a basket with a gingham serviette. Before serving, allow to cool to room temperature.

PUP-A-LEEKIE SOUP

AN OLD FAVOURITE from Scotland, this soup is perfect for that cold winter's evening when the puppy has just chewed up your last pair of slippers and pooed in the mathematical dead centre of your twist pile carpet.

INGREDIENTS

To serve 4	2 oz (50g) prunes
1 puppy	1 lb (500g) leeks, sliced
1 pint (¼ litre) hound stock	2 oz (50g) parsley, chopped

METHOD

Prepare and trim puppy. Place in a saucepan and add sliced leeks, prunes and hound stock. Simmer for three hours and serve piping hot, garnished with parsley.

HANDY HINT: For those of you suffering from any volatile bowel condition, we recommend you exclude the prunes from this recipe.

P et cuisine owes much to its founder Sir Reginald Bunty
Montcreif, Reg to his legion of friends and admirers. Master of
Hounds and tireless crusader for the rights of pet munchers
worldwide, Sir Reginald created many a classic dish and many
a cunning machine (see opposite page).

His flashes of inspiration were often preceded by curious fits of
uncontrollable twitching. Following one particularly nasty attack in
the winter of 1931, the entire pack of fox hounds belonging to the
South Downshire Hunt disappeared and the finger of suspicion was
pointed at Sir Reginald.

So began the first of many stretches spent in various institutions.

Branded a menace to society and a threat to every decent law
abiding pet in the land by some, and a genius by others, Sir Reg met
an untimely end in a mysterious incident in 1958 involving two Jack

Russell Terriers and a bazooka, sadly passing on before he could cap his life's work by bringing to fruition that orgasmic pinnacle of the Montcreif craft, Crufts Supreme Champion (see page 50).

Right. Sir Reginald Bunty Montcreif's patent "Bunny-To-Burger in Ten Seconds Flat", machine.

Below. A cutaway drawing completed shortly before an arrest showing the intricate mechanics of the machine. (Sir Reg stands by in stylish head gear, ready to crank the handle.)

BUNNY BURGERS

ACCESS TO A Montcreif "Bunny-to-Burger" machine would be useful for this popular snack but if one cannot be found we suggest you try an exploding "Nitro Carrot", available from all good novelty shops.

INGREDIENTS

To serve 1

1 rabbit, nitroed and finely chopped

2 large crusts of white thick sliced bread

1 small onion, finely chopped

1 large spoonful of Rumanian mustard (not suitable for children under 16)

METHOD

Combine chopped rabbit and onion, form into patti and deep fry in lard for ten minutes or until an attractive dark, gun metal grey colour. Toss onto bread crusts and donning a pair of industrial gloves, carefully cover with Rumanian mustard taking care to keep away from any naked flame. Best served as an open sandwich with a hearty pint of cold water and decorated with fluffy tail piece.

BUDGIE-ON-A-BUN

HERE WE HAVE the snacking version of the more ambitious Parrot-on-a-Loaf. Quick and simple, the dish has the added bonus that it can be enjoyed in uncanny silence, free from the continual whistling, chattering, bell-ringing, millet crunching and general clatter that was so much a hall mark of the family meal times before the feathered fiend met his maker.

INGREDIENTS

To serve 1

1 budgie, plucked and dressed

1 soft bread roll topped with bird seed (for which you'll have no more use)

1 twirl of Alaskan mayonnaise

salt, to taste

METHOD

Grill bird until crisp, salt liberally and place in bun. Decorate with mayonnaise twirl and a few left over feathers.

Serve on a small square of cage bottom sandpaper.

Ronaldo's
T·I·P ❶

I'm often asked how to stretch a small bird such as a canary to feed a family of four. Well, one way is to stuff the 2oz bird with 6 ½lb of sage and onion stuffing. This can be tricky but if you follow my four easy stages, success will be assured.

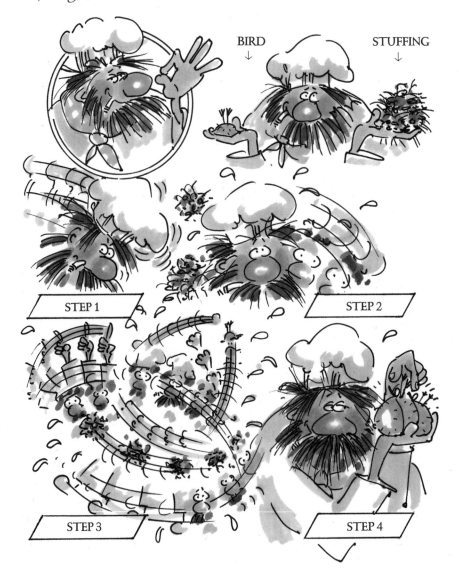

WASTE NOT WANT NOT

There are many handy side benefits available to the dedicated pet muncher and shown above are just four of the countless bits and bobs that can become decorative and useful additions to any home.

1. A stylish mogg hat for those cold winter mornings.

2. A trend-setting Rottweiller Rug for the house proud.

3. An attractive Elk Hound umbrella stand.

4. Have your cake and eat it with a stuffed memento of the family pet.

THE BRAT FACTOR

Dealing with a bout of persistent interrogation from a child as to the whereabouts of say, the family cat, can be a pain in the griddle. The inquisitive child should never be under-estimated. The more observant amongst them may even be astute enough to remark on the uncanny resemblance to the unfortunate beast, born by the Sunday roast. Don't panic! Several handy excuses can be made to placate a tiny mind in turmoil. One of my personal favourites is 'Felix is out to lunch'. This one not only amuses the adult diners but often serves to stem the flood of inquisitive juvenile banter.

Whatever happens, never let a snivelling, hysterical brat come between you and your enjoyment of a first class dish. If the disruption persists, turn to page 7, figure 3 and apply the same technique to the offending child!

26

KITTEN KRISP N' SOUR KRAUT

 THIS DISH WAS born in the trenches of France seventy odd years ago as both British and German troops were faced with yet another Bully Beef Christmas.

Who will ever forget the festive fraternisation as Tommy Atkins and Fritz, forgetting for a moment their little differences, rounded up trench kittens to produce that magical Anglo-Prussian military mega-classic, Kitten Krisp n' Sour Kraut, a dish delicious enough to bring a smile to the face of a man with the severest case of Trenchfoot. The dish became a year round favourite and was known in British trenches as Cat and Chips and in the French trenches as Petit Chat au Gruyère avec Fruits de Mer et Caviar Suspirus.

Nothing could be simpler.

INGREDIENTS

To serve 3

2 or 3 kittens, prepared and dressed

4 large cabbages

4 pints (2 litres) of water

1 bottle of vinegar

METHOD

Chop cabbage and place with kittens on large steel platter. Splash with water and scorch with MK. 9 Flamethrower until a crisp golden brown. Sprinkle with vinegar and serve in a billy can or steel helmet.

THE MAIN COURSES

Surely nothing can be more nourishing and wholesome for the larger than average family than a larger than average helping of family dog, so we start this chapter with the perennial favourite Rib of Rover. Over the years such main course recipes have become a popular Sunday roast for the bigger gathering and a familiar sight at our motorway cafes as coach loads of football hooligans cheerfully tuck into huge helpings with their Stanley knives.

There are several interesting and fun ways to prepare a hound for the pot, two of which I've touched upon in this book. The technique

employed opposite is entitled "The Dog that Died of Shame", and requires that the unfortunate hound be forced into the back of a pea green Reliant three-wheeler and driven slowly in full view of the other neighbour-hood dogs. In no time at all, a once proud hound will have succumbed to heart-stopping shame. His journey will end in the kitchen.

Another popular technique is the "Plywood-Cutout-Bitch-in-Heat-Nailed-to-a-Skateboard" method, which is described in detail on page 40.

RIB OF ROVER

A TRULY UNCOMPLICATED meal enjoyed the world over. The collar, lead and identity disc of the deceased hound should be arranged prettily about the carcass to add visual impact, but do remember to remove these before carving as mistakes have been made and the lead and collar, particularly if studded, are extremely difficult to chew.

INGREDIENTS

To feed a large family or coach load

35 to 45lb (17 to 22kg) hound, prepared and dressed

7lb (3.5kg) onions

3lb (1.5kg) butter

4lb (2kg) Madagascan passion nuts

1 gallon (4 litres) heavily salted water

43 stock cubes

METHOD

Place hound in a very large roasting tray, throw in a handful of everything, dot with butter, splash in the water and place in pre-heated oven at 375°F (190°C), Gas Mark 5 for 13 to 15 hours.

Cook's TIP: Try marinating the carcass in 7 or 8 gallons (32 litres) of Headbangers Premium Lager for 36 hours prior to cooking, but please don't attempt to drive a motor vehicle or operate machinery for at least 24 hours after consumption.

TRUSSED PARROT AU VIN

WHAT A STIRRING sight this dish makes. A parrot cooked to a crisp, trussed with piano wire, mounted upon a plinth and decorated with diced turnip, the whole towering above a calm European wine lake on which boats of mange-tout sail back and forth like a tiny green Armada. A French pièce-de-resistance for that special dinner party.

INGREDIENTS

A romantic dinner for 2

1 large parrot

2 large turnips

1 handful of mange-tout

1 gallon (4 litres) European semi-Rosé wine

1lb (500g) butter

METHOD

Pluck, dress and truss parrot. Dot with butter and roast in a pre-heated oven at 400°F (200°C), Gas Mark 6. Dice turnips and boil with mange-tout until very, very soft. Remove parrot when crisp and place on plinth, feet to the ceiling. Fill base with Euro wine, decorate parrot with diced turnip and float mange-tout on wine lake.

COOK'S TIP: Go for the parrot that's spent its life showering insults and obscenities on one and all as a feeling of great satisfaction at getting even can be experienced at the trussing stage.

THE PRINCE OF DARKNESS

For notoriety, one domestic pet stands furry head and shoulders above all others. I speak of the ferret. A more aggressive irritable flea-bag of a beast would be hard to imagine. Therefore, these two pages should be studied closely before attempting Ferret Flambé (overleaf).

Always remember the ferret is a yob.

Almost totally fearless.

Faster than a bullet.

But thankfully not invulnerable.

Ronaldo's
T·I·P ❷

I've had many many unpleasant experiences with ferrets, one of them accounting for my voice being slightly higher pitched than other men of comparable age. Follow my advice below if a ferret recipe calls for stuffing.

. . . Before attempting such an operation.

GGGRRRRRR!!

. . . Make sure.

. . . Your ferret is absolutely defunct!

FERRET FLAMBÉ

HAVING SURVIVED AN undoubtedly violent encounter with the main ingredient in this dish, some cooks are apt to be very heavy handed with the petroleum spirit called for in the recipe. Do use sparingly and try not to succumb to the overwhelming urge for revenge.

INGREDIENTS

To serve 2

1 ferret

4lb (2kg) thyme and parsley stuffing (see page 33)

3lb (1.5kg) Danish onions

1 bottle of olive oil

3 gallons (12 litres) Four star petroleum spirit

3 gallons (12 litres) water

METHOD

Dress and prepare ferret. Force thyme and parsley into the appropriate receptical. Peel and chop onions and place around ferret on a steel dish. Remove outdoors, to open ground. Baste with olive oil, marinate in petrol and toss on lighted match. When mushroom-shaped cloud reaches 400 feet, douse with water and serve with onions immediately.

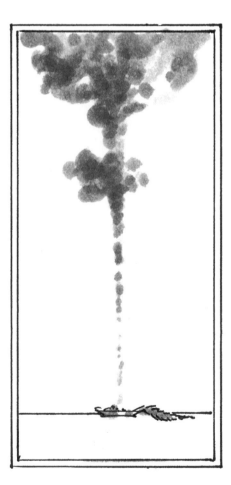

HANGING AND AGEING

The quality of many dishes can be improved by hanging and ageing. Above we see a fine example of the art, in the cellar of Sir Reginald Bunty Montcreif. The entire pack of hounds belonging to the South Downshire Hunt hang from the ceiling in a glorious state of suspended animation.

A GYMKHANA, A BEER TENT, A COUPLE OF DRINKS AND A GREAT DISH IS BORN

The story goes that several years ago an inquisitive pony wandered into the rear of a beer tent at a gymkhana in the south of England. There, it happened upon several leaking barrels of Brainsquashers Triple X Lager. What with it being a very hot day and the pony being very thirsty, one thing led to another and before long the animal was hoofless. Three hours and four gallons later, it staggered from the tent into the paddock, where, after brawling with several other ponies, it allowed it's young rider to saddle up and direct it's drunken energies towards the jumping competition. With the Brainsquashers on board, it not only went around the course in record time but cleared the final jump by 8 feet! Immediately after entering the winner's enclosure, the unfortunate beast was set upon by four dozen hysterically horsey children who patted him with such enthusiasm he never recovered.

Dragging itself painfully once more towards the beer tent, the pony made it only as far as the barbecue where it expired from the effects of severe patting and an appalling hangover.

The proprietor of the barbecue, always with an eye for the main chance and a weakness for meat marinated in lager, organised a lightning quick operation, and before the search which had been mounted for the beast by it's distraught young owner could bear fruit, Children's Pony à la Prix de L'Arc de Triomphe was created.

...WHEN I TAKE YOU OUT IN THE SURREY WITH THE FRINGE ON TOP....

Ronaldo's T·I·P ❸

When dealing with ponies, beware of what we in the business call "The Smart Ass".
The "Unsaddling at 30 Miles Per Hour Routine",
illustrated below, is a typically spiteful tactic employed by such a beast.

CHILDREN'S PONY À LA PRIX DE L'ARC DE TRIOMPHE

I ALWAYS LOOK back with mouth-watering fondness to that spell-binding scene from the film "The Godfather" as a gentleman is surprised by a hearty helping of this dish as his breakfast in bed. However, I still puzzle at the thankless reaction displayed by this lucky person and have since wondered if good food is often wasted on the uninitiated. Here's the recipe in all its glory.

INGREDIENTS

To serve a horse box full of diners

1 pony (11–12 hands)

2 large parsnips

1 small onion

9 gallons (36 litres) Brainsquashers Lager

1 gallon (4 litres) hoof oil

METHOD

Having marinated overnight in lager, dress, bone and prepare the pony. Baste with hoof oil and toss bodily onto large mound of glowing charcoal. Barbecue, turning frequently until golden brown. Serve with boiled parsnip and the small onion. Decorate with rosettes and trophies. NB If charcoal is hard to find, burn the horse box.

A FEW WORDS ABOUT NOUVELLE CUISINE

NO! NO! NYET! NIEN! NO WAY!

I'm often asked, "What about nouvelle cuisine à la pet?" and my stock answer is always, "What about it?".

The pathetic spread below is a typical product of the new breed of chef attempting to infiltrate the ranks of pet lovers. It was described on the menu of the bourgeois establishment where it was on offer, as a spit roasted cage bird set on a paddy field of wild rice, bordered by a jungle of greenery nestling at the foot of two soaring mountains of creamed pommes topped with two olive groves!

We leave you to make up your own minds and can add little other than to urge all dedicated pet lovers to say an emphatic no! non! nyet! nien! and no way! to nouvelle cuisine.

NAILING YOUR DOG
THE "PLYWOOD-CUTOUT-BITCH-IN-HEAT-NAILED-TO-A-SKATEBOARD" METHOD

Depicted below is an extremely clever way to outwit even the sharpest of hounds. It requires that you cut from plywood a model of a bitch in heat. Suitably painted and nailed to a skateboard, on which the wheels have been well oiled, it makes an extremely attractive target for the randy mut, who, in a state of happy abandon passes from procreation to devastation in 5 seconds flat.

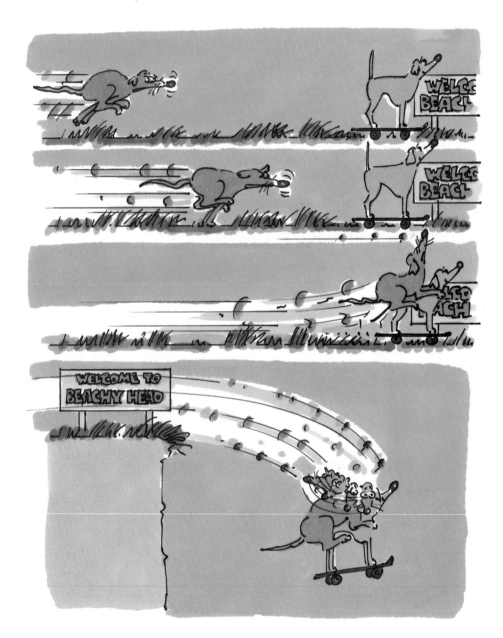

101 DALMATIONS WITH 76 TROMBONES POMME FLAMBÉ

A RECIPE INSPIRED by the majesty of two epic films. Suitable for the large banquet, this splendid dish is an awesome sight when laid out, each hound nose to tail and 300 eager diners straining at the leash to get started.

This dish is so popular amongst the banqueting fraternity that the author doubts there are 101 Dalmations left in the country, but should the opportunity to acquire them present itself, don't hesitate to take advantage of a once in a life time opportunity.

INGREDIENTS

To serve up to 303

101 Dalmations

76 sacks of King Edward potatoes

10lb (5kg) onions

14lb (7kg) beetroot

1 gallon (4 litres) olive oil

25 cloves of garlic

10 bottles of brandy

2 handfuls of chilli peppers

48 gallons (192 litres) of water

salt and pepper, to taste

METHOD

Dress and prepare hounds and place in 17ft. Steamboat (see page 7), along with the 48 gallons (192 litres) of water, salt, peeled onions, beetroot and potatoes. Simmer gently for 6 to 7 hours. Remove potatoes and mash with two handfuls of chilli peppers.

Remove Dalmations from the steamboat, rub with garlic cloves, brush with olive oil and brown with a blow torch.

Here comes the tricky bit. Sculpt 76 trombones from the potato mix and arrange between the hounds together with the onions and beetroot as shown in the illustration. Pour the brandy into the trombones and as a final flourish set fire to them and serve piping hot. A real show stopper!

RODENT MEDLEY

THIS IS AN extremely tasty recipe containing a balanced mixture of mouse, gerbil, hamster and the more 'gamey' guinea pig. Very popular in canteens attached to research laboratories, this medley contains something for everybody.

INGREDIENTS

To serve up to 2

2 mice

1 gerbil

1 hamster

½ guinea pig

1 large spring cabbage

4 garlic cloves

1 pint (½ litre) rodent stock

½ bottle olive oil

METHOD

Dress rodents and toss into a pan containing very hot olive oil. When sealed, add rodent stock, chopped vegetables, garlic cloves and simmer gently for 1½ hours.

Arrange on a large platter in ascending order of size, decorate with a rodent wheel and serve immediately.

HOME FREEZING

An animal will keep for months if frozen and the most effective way to do this with a domestic pet is to freeze it with fear. We all know the feeling! Below are two of the most popular methods.

1. "Willy the Wimp" in trap 2 has been frozen, literally dead in his tracks as a huge, stuffed hare, nailed to a trolley by his hungry owner has been sent back around the track. This amusing but deadly practical joke is known in racing circles as "The Hare's Revenge".

∴ "A BILL TO CASTRATE ALL TOM CATS BY THE HOUSE BRICK METHOD WAS PASSED UNANIMOUSLY BY PARLIAMENT TODAY....."

2. The "Makeatape" method. Make a tape to sound like a news broadcast and place in a radio cassette player to attract the attention of your passing mogg. In no time, he'll be ready for the fridge.

CAPTURING A SHIP'S CAT

STIR FRIED GINGER WITH TOM

MUCH LOVED ON the South China Sea, the most difficult part of this recipe is catching its main ingredient, ship's cat. Ten years before the mast can turn a moggie into a very shrewd character indeed. The ginger Tom on the left is too clever by half to end up in the ship's wok but success can be had with the less experienced puss.

INGREDIENTS

To serve a galley full

1 ship's cat

4 packets of ship's biscuits

1 box of hard tack

2 large onions

1 large ginger root

loads and loads of noodles

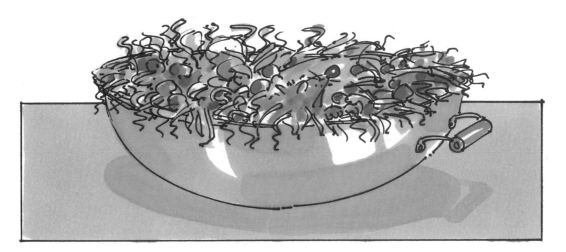

METHOD

The older ship's cat can be very tough, so much hacking and flailing with a 12-inch cleaver may be required to reduce it to bite-sized chunks. Chop onion and drill hard tack into 1 inch cubes. Slice ginger and toss the lot into a hot, oiled wok. Add loads of noodles and stir fry briskly. Drill or smash ship's biscuit until crumbled and sprinkle in. Place in bowls and serve with segments of fresh lime as a hedge against scurvy.

CHIHUAHUA CHILLI

A VERY HOT dish from Mexico, land of song and strange, shivering little dogs with large heads and even larger eyes. On no account allow this cute little animal to appeal to your sensitivity.

He'll try everything from placing his tail between his legs and shivering uncontrollably, to attempting to stare you out with large, oil puddle eyes. Be strong! Fight back the tears and remember, a chef's got to do what a chef's got to do.

INGREDIENTS

To serve 1

1 Chihuahua	1 pint (½ litre) of water
2 tins of red kidney beans	olive oil
2 onions	loads and loads of chilli

METHOD

Reduce Chihuahua to bite-size chunks by dividing carefully into two equal pieces. Toss into pan and fry with onions until brown. Add water, beans and chilli. Simmer for 1 hour and serve in a large earthenware bowl. As a finishing touch, decorate the bowl as shown with the animal's little tartan walking coat and silk bow.

COOK'S TIP: This dish is red hot and should not be given to children or attempted by persons suffering from a heart condition or high blood pressure.

SIR REG STRIKES

A classic manoeuvre, resulting in disaster for the monkey, perpetrated by Sir Reginald Bunty Montcreif. He presses the button opening the service hatch of a barrel organ belonging to a gentleman who had plagued cinema queues in west London for a decade.

As the music and dance grind to a halt, Sir Reg is given a standing ovation by the cinema goers.

GROUND ORGAN GRINDER'S MONKEY

ONCE IN THE front rank of show business, the organ grinder's monkey has thankfully become quite rare in the world of entertainment. However, some furry hoofers can still be found in the odd back water, gyrating to a mind-bendingly tuneless barrel organ, so keep your eyes peeled and your ears covered.

INGREDIENTS

To serve 4	1 handful of powdered mace
4lb (2kg) of ground monkey	2 eggs
4 sheets of leaf gelatine	2lb (1kg) of carrot

METHOD

Prepare carrots, dice and along with the other ingredients, place in a large pot and cover with salted water. Bring to the boil and reduce for 1 hour. Cool and pour mixture into decorative jelly mould, and allow to set. Decorate with top hat and cane.

THE DISH WE CAN ONLY DREAM OF

Here we see "Winifred Blue Rinse Supremo Eleganza", (top) one of the many thoroughbred hounds who over the years have held the coveted title, Crufts Supreme Champion. What a spell binding centrepiece she'd make for the dream dish opposite!

Above. A police photograph showing a triumph of ingenuity! A front and back view of Sir Reginald's exploding rosette. Note the five sticks of gelignite and brass alarm clock cunningly concealed on the reverse side.

(Sir Reg was arrested before the rosette could make it's mark on the hound and hence an historic contribution to pet cuisine.)

CRUFTS CHAMPION SUPREME

SIR REG STRUGGLED all his days to bring this dish, his life's dream to fruition, but due to a combination of bad luck and tight security he was never able to infiltrate the closed ranks of sickeningly devoted owners and showers who make up the annual lurid spectacle we know as Crufts Dog Show. As this recipe has never been attempted, the quantities and ingredients can only be guessed at.

INGREDIENTS

To serve ?

1 Supreme Champion	1 small turnip
4 lb (2kg) potatoes	2 lb (2kg) butter
2 pints (1 litre) of hound stock	cornflour
4 lb (2kg) carrots	salt, to taste

METHOD

Prepare and dress the hound, dot with butter, sprinkle with salt and place in pre-heated oven at 350°F (180°C), Gas Mark 4. Boil up vegetables and set aside. When hound is crispy brown, add juices to stock, boil up, thicken with cornflour and pour over carcass. Arrange vegetables around the hound, decorate with Supreme Champ rosette, and mount the whole lot on a winner's rostrum.

THE MAGIC OF MAGNIFICATION

Unlike it's cousin the Siamese Fighting Fish, the little known Fresh Water Fighting Fish has one major drawback. Fully grown it measures only .05 centimetres in length. Hence it tends only to mug and squabble with its own kind, steering well clear of other fish who consider it a laughing stock. However, this mindless miniature mass of malevolence can be used to good effect in providing the main ingredients for the recipe on the opposite page.

1. The unfortunate animal being taunted.

2. By sliding its bowl in front of the aquarium, thereby employing the "Magnification Technique", the insignificant speck instantly becomes a huge, heaving mass of cold blooded evil and the tables are turned on the taunters.

NEPTUNE'S BOUNTIFUL HARVEST ON A GREAT BARRIER REEF OF FLUFFY RICE N' FOSTERS

THIS RECIPE FROM the tropical waters around Australia is full of Antipodean promise. Exotic, mystical, enigmatic and incredibly filling, it provides a pleasant change from that traditional Australian breakfast, A Fridge Full of Fosters.

INGREDIENTS

To serve 2

1 doz assorted tropical fish (nothing brown or spikey)

4 garlic cloves

1 gallon (4 litres) of Fosters

large quantity of fluffy rice

½ bottle of olive oil

1 lemon

METHOD

Boil rice until soft, drain and in a large, deep bowl, form into a shape resembling the Great Barrier Reef. Pour in gallon of Fosters. Fry fish in olive oil with garlic. When cooked remove from pan and float onto the Reef. Serve with a squirt of lemon.

Handy HINT: A smaller snack version of this recipe exists, called Neptune's Bountiful Harvest in a Billabong of Fluffy Rice n' Fosters.

CAPITALIST RUNNING DOG

A GRAND BANQUETING feast from the canteen of the "Great Hall of the People". Complex and inscrutable, it was such a great picnic favourite on "The Long March" that it is estimated 75% of all dogs living along the route vanished in the wok.

INGREDIENTS

To serve a platoon	2 onions
1 medium-size dog	extremely large quantity of rice
loads of beansprouts	3 scoops Mono Sodium Glutamate

METHOD

Dress and prepare dog. Sprinkle with two scoops of Mono Sodium Glutamate and place on spit above charcoal grill. Boil rice until soft, throw into wok and stir fry along with beansprouts, onion and remaining scoop of Mono Sodium Glutamate. When cooked to a lively shade of Red, position dog as shown on a large platter and arrange rice, vegetables and little red books at the animal's feet. The whole dish is then mounted on a trolley and pushed the length of the banqueting table.

GRAND CHRISTMAS LUNCH

"Christmas comes but once a year and
when it comes Pet munchers cheer."

One of the high points of our culinary calendar, Christmas is looked forward to by us all with mouth-watering anticipation.

Not for us the battery reared chicken, but rather the free range hound who's roamed at will the streets and alleyways of the neighbourhood uncaged.

Not for us the polypropylene turkey, frozen into submission on the supermarket meat counter, but more the unfettered corn fed gerbil and the well travelled pigeon, home to roost from 2000 feet (see overleaf).

Here's a Christmas Lunch we can all enjoy with a clear conscience, safe in the knowledge that the principal ingredients have been lucky enough to avoid the factory farm.

BIRDSTRIKE SURPRISE

To serve a normal family of 4

Our lunch begins with a dish that's been a favourite for many years around busy airports. It's main advantages are that the meal comes plucked and ready cooked so there's no mess, and no washing up.

It involves releasing a flock of homing pigeons close to an airport runway, and keeping one's fingers crossed for a bird strike. Be ready with a plate and do try to coincide the release with the arrival or departure of an Air France plane as this airline tends to take just that little bit more time and trouble with the end product.

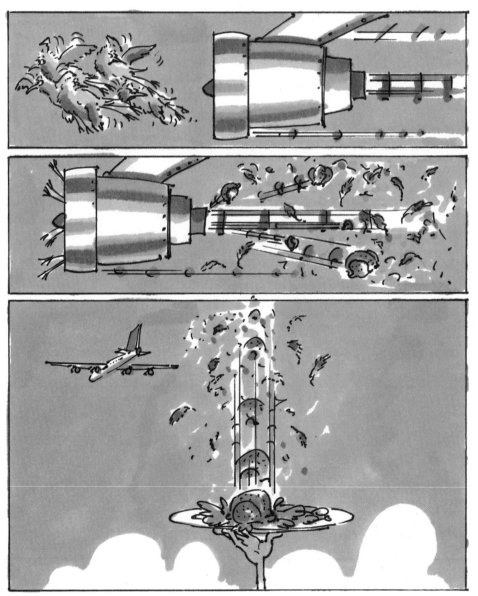

NODDING DOG

OUT OF THE car onto the table, this grand Christmas main course is inspired by those amusing ornaments that so tastefully grace the rear window of many a swanky automobile. As it's eyes light up, so will the faces of your children at this special time of year.

INGREDIENTS

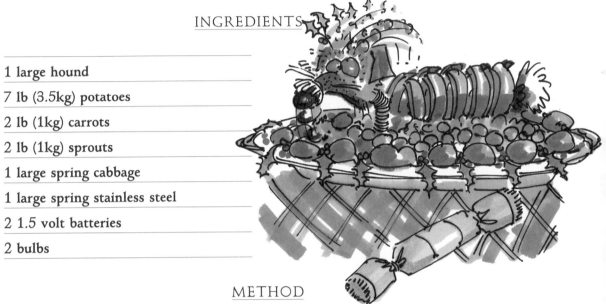

1 large hound

7 lb (3.5kg) potatoes

2 lb (1kg) carrots

2 lb (1kg) sprouts

1 large spring cabbage

1 large spring stainless steel

2 1.5 volt batteries

2 bulbs

METHOD

Prepare hound, baste with oil and place in preheated oven at 300°F (150°C), Gas Mark 3 for 3 hours. *Do not* cook steel spring bulbs or batteries.

Prepare vegetables and boil until soft. Place potatoes around the hound and roast for 40 minutes. When done, arrange hound as shown in illustration, mount on the spring and wire up battery to bulbs to make an eyecatching festive centrepiece.

GERBIL FOOL

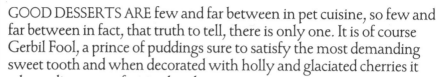

GOOD DESSERTS ARE few and far between in pet cuisine, so few and far between in fact, that truth to tell, there is only one. It is of course Gerbil Fool, a prince of puddings sure to satisfy the most demanding sweet tooth and when decorated with holly and glaciated cherries it makes a spectacular ending to our fesitive lunch.

INGREDIENTS

2 gerbils	2 eggs
4 gills (½ litre) of milk	2 glaciated cherries
1 lb (500g) Apricot jam	1 cup of desiccated coconut
8 sponge cakes	1 lb (500g) caster sugar
1 bottle of Dark Rum	

METHOD

Prepare and trim gerbils. Cut sponge cakes in half, mix with eggs, milk, sugar, and jam. Add the bottle of rum and stir briskly. Stand in a pan of hot water and add gerbils when mixture begins to thicken. Decorate with holly, sprinkle with desiccated coconut, place a glaciated cherry on each little nose and serve.

WARNING: Having eaten this dessert some diners may break into spontaneous song. This is just the effects of the rum and there should be no cause for concern.

OFFAL-ON-A-WAFFLE

OVER THE YEARS, chefs concerned about waste have developed a dish using all the odds and sods left over after the Yuletide festivities. This recipe is a great favourite with the kids, and I for one look forward to the day when the "Offal-on-a-Waffle-Take away" is a familiar sight in our high streets.

INGREDIENTS

To serve a normal family of 4

all kitchen leftovers

½ lb (225g) flour

2 eggs

dash of milk

1 oz (25g) of butter

baking powder

salt and pepper, to taste

METHOD

Gather leftovers together and grind to a fine paste. Add salt and pepper, form into a ball and deep fry for 30 minutes. Mix flour, eggs, milk, butter and baking powder together into a batter. Using a waffle iron, cook until golden brown. Place Offal on the Waffle and serve with chips and a coke.

A SELECTION OF WINES

As a general rule when choosing alcohol to accompany your meal remember, red with fur, white with feather, lager with anything and you won't go far wrong. Listed below are a few firm favourites I've grown to love and respect over the years. From the gently fragrant Edelweiss Petal Wine fighting out of the rolling alpine meadows of Switzerland to Rouge People's Collective Farm Product No 17, that menacing and thunderously awesome bottled sludge from Albania.

Here is a selection we can heartily recommend to the pet lover.

1. COBBER VALLEY RED

From Australia, a cheeky number with a mystic whiff of the outback. Imported into England where it's known as "Convict's Revenge", this is excellent with Rodent.

2. CHATEAU ARTY FARTY

A mighty, immensely deep, crusty, enigmatic, heavenly bodied wine from France. Ecstatically joyful one minute, surrendering to a raging undercurrent of cosmic sadness the next, this titanic red is excellent with Children's Pony à la Prix de L'Arc de Triomphe (see page 38).

3. BERNARD PLONKER WINE-IN-A-MUG

From Silican Valley, California this is a true hi-tech wine, computer controlled throughout its production. Hugely hygienic, immensely crisp and fabulously clinical, it also kills 99% of all household germs.

4. EDELWEISS PETAL WINE

A delicate, fruity altogether efficient little wine from that happy-go-lucky, laugh a minute nation of people, the Swiss. Not so much a gnome of Zurich but more a giant of Geneva, this white is perfect with Parrot.

5. ROUGE PEOPLE'S COLLECTIVE FARM PRODUCT NO 17 IN A BOX

After a hard day's work, how relaxing to come home, sink into your favourite chair, take a few pre dinner sips of this majestic wine and succumb to a staggering series of electrifying halucinations culminating in the classic dance of the dragons. Rocket fuel, toilet cleaner and nail varnish remover to some, its wine to the connoisseur and fab with Ferret.

RESTAURANT GUIDE

Sadly only the tip of the pet cuisine iceberg stands proudly above the surface of a chips-with-everything-sea. The rest is hidden in Davy Jones's Locker, refusing to rise up from the depths and bare its furry chest. Specialist restaurants are therefore few and far between but happily some do exist, struggling for a place on the culinary map. The top three are detailed here.*

THE CHEEK BY JOWEL

A friendly three paw family run hotel restaurant specialising in rodent dishes. Rat-in-a-Basket is always available at the bar and an extensive wine list includes the rare Chateau du Pup. 🐾🐾🐾

OLD MOTHER MCDOUGAL'S PET PANTRY

The kids will love this two paw mobile fast food establishment situated in a lay-by on the A49. Renowned for its Offal-on-a-Waffle and generous helpings of Gerbil Fool, the diners are often entertained by Old Mother McDougal singing as she goes about her work at the griddle. 🐾🐾

BISTRO NIGEL MONTCRIEF

Owned and operated by the nephew of the legendary Sir Reginald, this is a truly splendid five paw restaurant. On a recent visit to this establishment with a loved one, it became clear as we bathed in the candle's glow, saw each other darkly through a huge pot of Venus Fly Traps, chewed our way through a classic Trussed Parrot au Vin, washing it down with a pint or two of Rouge People's Collective Farm Product No 17, that this would be, try as I might, an 'experience I would never forget'. 🐾🐾🐾🐾🐾

* Source *Fur n' Feather Quarterly.*

A WORD ABOUT REMORSE

Unfortunately, having wined and dined on the family pet, some owners are liable to feel sudden and uncontrollable pangs of remorse. *Remorse is a word that does not appear in the pet muncher's dictionary* and any compulsion to throw oneself into the microwave or gas oven should be resisted, as this course of action is far more painful than any feelings of guilt you may experience. If the sense of shame becomes overwhelming, we suggest you gather up the leftovers and salve your conscience by giving the unfortunate animal a decent burial.